THE WEEKEND
that changed
THE WORLD

THE WEEKEND
that changed
THE WORLD

David Littlewood

LIFESTREAM PUBLICATIONS

Nottingham, England

Copyright © 1992 Lifestream Publications
106/114 Talbot Street, Nottingham, England

First Edition 1992

ISBN 0 946586 05 5

Production and Printing in England for
LIFESTREAM PUBLICATIONS
by Nuprint Ltd, Station Road, Harpenden, Herts AL5 4SE.

CONTENTS

Foreword   7

Introduction   9

Part 1: FRIDAY MORNING...The Price is Paid   13

1   The Importance of the Cross   17
2   Why The Cross?   21
3   What The Cross Achieved   27
4   Justification by Faith   35
5   God's Sons   41

Part 2: SUNDAY COMES...Death is Conquered!   45

6   The Evidence   51
7   The Appearance of Jesus   63
8   The Importance of the Resurrection   67

Part 3: TODAY...Resurrection Life!   75

9   The New Birth   79
10 A Great Helper   83
11 God's Final Purpose   95

FOREWORD

Asked what he regarded as his greatest discovery, Sir James Young Simpson MD, the doctor accredited with the introduction of chloroform as an anaesthetic, gave an unexpected answer. It was Christ not chloroform. His reply was, "My greatest discovery was when I discovered what Christ could be to me."

If you have not yet joined Sir James in making life's greatest discovery, then I want to recommend this book as being a concise and clear treasure map. On the first page you will find that X marks the spot. Its philosophy is delightfully simple and uncomplicated. "Go straight to Christ through the Cross. Do not pass Go. Do not collect £200." No diversions. No delays. This guidebook is so uncomplicated that you may begin reading as a born sceptic but by the last page finish as a born again Christian.

The book's author was a physics teacher before becoming a minister. Physics is a branch of science concerned with the ultimate laws which govern the structure of the universe and forms of matter and energy and their interactions. Physics is about proofs, laws, and logic. The author has combined his training and skills as a teacher with his experience as a minister to explain how "through Christ Jesus the law of the

Spirit of life will set you free from the law of sin and death" (Rom 8:2).

If you have already joined Sir James and have discovered Christ as Saviour and Lord, this book will still bless you and strengthen you and provide you with sound wisdom and advice about the inexhaustible riches that are yours in Christ. Christianity is Christ and I am glad to recommend this book because it is all about Christ. And that is what life, real life, is all about—Christ, the Son of God. "He who has the Son has life; he who does not have the Son of God does not have life" (1 Jn 5:12).

COLIN WHITTAKER
Editor of *Redemption*

INTRODUCTION

The hot Indian sun beat down, turning the inside of the van in which we were travelling into a near furnace. I was glad when we arrived at the church in which we were to conduct the seminars. Here, a burly, courteous man welcomed me and helped me out of the van. Although I did not understand a word of his language, the radiance which shone from his face and the smile that nearly bisected his features told me that here was a fine Christian.

Imagine my surprise when I learned that this man had been, in fact, a convicted murderer! Years before he had killed a man in a jealous rage and been sent to prison. However, while he was behind bars a wonderful change had taken place: he had found Jesus Christ as his Saviour. Now love and joy replaced the bitterness and hatred which had caused him to kill.

That Indian pastor I met in Coimbatore is merely one of hundreds of people I have known whose lives have been radically changed, not by an experience of religion, but by the living Christ himself. All over the world today, people are finding the wonderful new life that Jesus promised when he said, "I have come that they might have life, and have it to the full".

As Christians we believe that the God of the Bible speaks to us primarily through the events of history, and in particular through the life of his Son, Jesus Christ; above all by what Jesus did for us by dying on the cross and rising again from the dead. What's more, Jesus' death and resurrection can make a radical difference to our lives today.

This book is written to acquaint people with the facts, both historical and theological, of that first Easter, and also to show how the living Christ can transform our lives today. It is important for us to know the facts and the way the Bible writers interpret them, not so that we can carry them in our heads, but so that they will make the radical difference to our lives that God intends.

It is the author's prayer that each person reading this book, whether an inquirer or committed Christian, may find the power of the risen Christ and the new lifestyle he offers us.

NOTE

To avoid cluttering the text, yet facilitate the reader's own study, some scripture references have been given in the "notes" at the end of each section.

Part 1

Friday Morning . . .
The Price Is Paid

Part 1

INTRODUCTION

In the gloom of the early morning the excited crowd gathered round the place of execution with all the morbid sense of anticipation that depraved human nature could muster for these occasions. Well named, "The Place of the Skull",[1] this desolate piece of rock had seen the last dying agonies of many who had dared to defy the might of Rome.

Soon two men, thieves by the inscription hung round their necks, were led forward, and laid naked upon two crosses. They screamed and cursed as the nails were driven in and the crosses unceremoniously jolted into position.

However, the real interest for the crowd came with the third man, whom the soldiers were to make the centrepiece for their barbaric ritual. A young carpenter from Nazareth, who had gained a reputation as a prophet and miracle worker was dragged forward, his face and body a mass of blood from the merciless scourging he had already received. The charge Pilate had cynically placed round his neck was "The King of the Jews".[2]

As he was brutally nailed and the cross hoisted into position, amid the taunts and mockery of the crowd, he was heard to say words that were to become associated with Christians of all generations: "Father, forgive them, for they do not know what they are doing."[3] And as he died amid the gathering darkness, few realised that the instrument of torture which bore the weight of his pain-wracked body would become the symbol of hope, victory and redemption for millions.

For when the carpenter cried, "It is finished,"[4] he did not just mean his life was gone, but that the work of redemption was completed by his death. Now the gap which had existed between a holy God and sinful man would be forever bridged by the arms outstretched on that cross; and as if to illustrate the point, the veil in the temple, which symbolised man's separation from God was torn in two.[5] The price had been paid. Jesus by his work had done the impossible: God and sinners were reconciled to each other.

1

The Importance of The Cross

The cross of Jesus is absolutely central to the New Testament; it is mentioned directly more than 175 times. All four Gospels are structured round it. They are not biographies; they have, in fact, aptly been called "Passion narratives with extended introductions". Each Gospel climaxes with the death of Christ; and in each one the death and resurrection of Jesus take up a disproportionate number of pages. Fundamental to their title "Gospels" (which means "good news") is the good news of what God has done in redeeming sinful man through the death of his Son.

Moreover, the Gospels and the other New Testament documents do not see the death of Jesus as a tragic miscarriage of justice or even a brave man dying for a just cause. From the birth of the church the apostles made it clear that Jesus was handed over to die "by God's set purpose and foreknowledge" (Acts 2:23). The cross is not seen as an act of lawless men but rather an act of God, planned from before time began.[6] The death of Christ was therefore anticipated and predicted by many of the the Old Testament prophets,[7] and it was the subject of Moses and Elijah's conversation with Jesus on the Mount of Transfiguration.[8]

What's more, Jesus is seen to go willingly to his death as something he would accomplish. For most men death means the end of accomplishment, the end of hopes. Even the pious Hezekiah, when faced with death, "wept bitterly".[9] Yet Jesus spoke freely about his death to his disciples on many occasions (Mt 16:21–28), and gave a stern rebuke to Peter for suggesting any other course of action. We see Jesus setting his face towards Jerusalem where he knew he would die, and, when the time was nearly upon him, saying that "the hour has come for the Son of Man to be glorified" (Jn 12:23).

The New Testament therefore portrays Jesus, not as a helpless victim of man's cruelty, but an active participant in what he knew to be his chief purpose in coming into the world—to die on the cross. For Jesus the cross is the means by which he would draw all men to himself.[10]

This is important in an age in which spiritual lightweights are inclined to ignore or even deny the relevance of the cross. The message, they say, of Christianity does not lie in the barbarous theme of blood sacrifice. Rather it is in the life and teaching of Jesus, the fact that he showed God loves us and pointed the way for us to reform ourselves. If we only follow Jesus' example there will be liberation, "peace on earth and goodwill towards men."

This is far from the attitude of the Gospel writers and the early church. Paul was a mighty intellectual, one of the ablest men who has ever lived. Yet when preaching the Gospel he had but one theme: Christ and him crucified.[11] It did not matter to Paul that the Jews stumbled over the idea of a crucified Messiah, or that the Greeks thought he was mad for preaching such things.[12] It was "of first importance" to his message that "Christ died for our sins according to the Scriptures" (1 Cor 15:4). The heart of his Gospel was that

"Christ Jesus came into this world to save sinners" (1 Tim 1:15).

For all his learning and Jewish nationalistic fervour, Paul believed he had found the answer to life not in the rigours of the Jewish religion, nor in abstract philosophical and intellectual debate, but in the death of the carpenter of Nazareth. It was this death that gave him the power to live, and his boast was not in his intellect, his nationality or his religious inheritance; rather, he tells the Galatians, "May I never boast except in the cross of our Lord Jesus Christ, through which the world has been crucified to me and I to the world" (Gal 6:14).

The power of the cross changed Saul the bigoted, Jewish zealot to Paul the apostle. It was the preaching of the cross by Paul and many others like him that brought new hope to a dying Roman civilisation. And it is the power of that same cross today that can make a difference in the lives of men and women stricken by the terrible burdens and pressures of our modern, materialistic culture. Through the cross we can gain a new life; as Bunyan's Pilgrim said, "He has given me life through his death."[13]

2

Why the Cross?

Sin

The wonder of the cross of Christ is that it addresses the fundamental problem of mankind—the fact of sin. Modern man, living in the post-Christian era, tends to view the human predicament as due to things outside of man himself; for example, poverty and lack of education or resources. If we could only put these things right, he thinks, there would be an end to quarrelling, wars and crime. Of course, when man has evolved to a higher form of life, he will realise the folly of his ways and all will be well!

The Bible, however, tells us that sin is the problem. Man was made in the image of God to live as the son of God, in loving harmony with both God and creation.[14] But Genesis 3 very clearly shows us that, by listening to the voice of the serpent (which we now know was Satan, the devil), man disobeyed God and in doing so lost his relationship with God. Sin entered the human race and man fell from being a creature free to perform the will of God into a creature bound by Satan, unable to have a relationship with God.

Fundamental to sin is ungodliness—living without God . And it is clear that man's state of ungodliness always leads to unrighteousness in his actions. Paul shows this very clearly in Romans 1:18–32, where although men "...knew (about) God, they neither

21

glorified him as God nor gave thanks to him, but their thinking became futile...." The result of this is seen in all forms of wrongdoing, including idol worship, adultery, homosexuality and lesbianism, greed and depravity, envy, strife, murder, deceit and malice. These are just a few of the horrible things mentioned, and they are to be found in every society, for sin is universal: "All have sinned and fall short of the glory of God" (Rom 3:23).

This fact of sin, which is obvious to the Christian, was not obvious in the ancient world where many people did not see themselves as sinners. Similarly, in our modern world, it is not uncommon to find people still propounding the theory that men are basically good. How they do it in the face of the devastating wars that have taken place this century, together with the crime, selfishness, adultery, cruelty, child abuse, violence and hooliganism that pervade our modern "civilisations" is a matter for amazement!

But God's verdict upon man is true: "every inclination of his heart is evil from childhood" (Gen 8:21), and the cross itself supplies a graphic illustration of this. Here was Jesus Christ, going about doing good and working miracles of healing and deliverance as a sign that God was with him. Did men honour him and follow him? No! They nailed him to a cross in order to silence him. Surely that is the final proof of the wickedness of man's heart—the fact that "Light has come into the world, but men preferred darkness instead of light because their deeds were evil" (Jn 3:19).

Has the world got any better since the time of Jesus? An intelligent young man at a sixth form question time recently asked me why God hadn't sent Jesus today when man was far more enlightened and would have accepted him. The simple answer to that is provided by the awful persecution of Christians throughout the world today. Jesus told his disciples that men would hate them for the same reason as they crucified him, because they do not know God.[15] For all our sophistication and learning, the world today is just as much gripped by sin as it ever was.

The Wrath of God

However, sin has far more serious consequences for man than even earthly disorder and suffering. For the Bible tells us that God is holy and cannot bear to look on sin.[16] Therefore it often speaks of the "wrath of God" towards sinners (Jn 3:36; Rom 1:18), not just in this life but in a life that will go on beyond the grave throughout eternity.

We must not forget that Jesus himself often spoke about hell as the place of endless torment where the fire never goes out (Mk 9:43, 45, 47). However much we might fear certain men who have power to kill our bodies (a reality in Jesus' day as today), how much more should we fear the God who has power to cast us into hell![17] In the parable of the rich man and Lazarus (Lk 16:19–31), Jesus' language in describing the unending agonies of the rich man cast into hell is extraordinarily vivid, as is that of his denunciation of the scribes and pharisees in which he asks them, "How can you escape being condemned to hell?" (Mt 23:33) If we believe Jesus' teaching, the reality of the judgment and wrath of God upon sin is unmistakable.

The New Testament as a whole views judgment both as a present reality and a future certainty. Hence, the man who will not believe in Jesus will not have to wait for the future judgment day—he stands condemned already before God.[18] This judgment will finally happen when we stand before God's judgment seat.[19] In contrast to much of what is taught today, God views us as responsible people and "each of us will have to give an account of himself to God" (Rom 14:12). That judgment will be absolutely fair, righteous and true. No-one will be able to take exception when condemned because God's judgment is always "based on truth" (Rom 2:2).

The Love of God

It was to rescue us from the terrible effects of sin—past, present and future, that Jesus came. For God is not just a God of absolute integrity, holiness and justice—but also a God of love. Since the Fall of man it was in the purpose of God to save man from sin.[20] To do this, one of Adam's race had to be found—one who had never sinned. But who? All men, as we have seen, are under the terrible power of sin. Even the best men who have lived—men like Abraham, David, and Daniel, were all its victims.

Therefore, since no man could be found to deal with sin, God did the mightiest thing that had ever been done—God became a man—Jesus Christ.[21] John tells us, "God so loved the world that he gave his one and only Son, that whoever believes on him shall not perish but have everlasting life" (Jn 3:16).

As Dr. Martyn Lloyd-Jones has observed:

When the problem of forgiving sins arose it was necessary that the Son of God should leave the courts of heaven and come to earth and be born as a babe, suffer the contradiction of sinners against Himself, be put to death and shed

His blood. It was the only way. Such is the difficulty raised by the problem of the forgiveness of sins.[22]

In his life on earth Jesus lived as no man has ever lived—in full and complete obedience to God. Even his enemies could find no fault with him: not the fanatical pharisees, nor the cruel Pilate, nor the cynical and corrupt Herod.[23] And these men were looking for an excuse to get rid of Jesus! He therefore, as a man, defeated the power of sin which had, until that time, reigned supreme on the earth. As a result of this he could have entered into heaven as a man, justified before God by the life he led. We see perhaps a glimpse of this on the Mount of Transfiguration, where Jesus' glory shines out; at that moment he could have ascended to heaven.[24]

However, we see from this moment him setting his face towards something very different—Calvary. For Jesus knew his Father's will for himself: "The Son of Man did not come to be served, but to serve, and to give his life as a ransom for many" (Mk 10:45). For, if it was by his sinless life that Jesus overcame sin for himself, it was at Calvary that he conquered sin for every man after him who would believe. What took him there? Nothing but the love of God for a fallen and helpless race.

3

What the Cross Achieved

Throughout the New Testament, the wonderful achievement of Christ's death is brought out by the use of "picture words"[25]—words that vividly portray what the cross has done for us. Most of them were everyday words in New Testament times, although their meaning is often obscure to us.

Sacrifice

Sacrifice is one such word. To us, sheltered as we are in the Western world, with our meat arriving in plastic containers, the thought of an animal being slaughtered and burnt seems almost revolting. I remember my primary school teacher deploring the ancient practice, saying that God much preferred live animals to dead ones!

However, the Bible makes it clear that sacrifice was not just allowed by God—it was always central to his plan from the beginning. God cannot just forgive sins as if they did not matter. Sin has violated his holy law and his righteousness demands that sin must be punished. The penalty of sin is death[26] and that penalty must be paid for God to remain true to his nature.

From the beginning the principle of sacrifice is found in the Bible.[27] An innocent victim (an animal) was taken and killed in the place of a guilty sinner. The animal was then burned on the altar as an offering to God, and the guilt of the sinner was pardoned. Sacrifice was formalised under the Old Testament Law,[28] to provide hope for the sinner and a focus for his faith. There were many differing sacrifices, but the same principle ran through them all—the innocent shedding its blood, giving its life, for the guilty.

However, all thinking men knew that "it is impossible for the blood of bulls and goats to take away sins" (Heb 10:4). In order to deal with sin in man, a sacrifice had to be found from among the race of men—an innocent victim to die for guilty men. The Old Testament sacrifices pointed the way to the great sacrifice for sin that was to come. And in Jesus God provided that sacrifice.

Calvary was therefore a sacrifice to God. Jesus did not die for his own sins (he was sinless) but for the sins of others. Isaiah vividly prophesied concerning Christ's death: "He was pierced for our transgressions, and crushed for our iniquities; the punishment that brought us peace was upon him, and by his wounds we are healed" (Is 53:5). Peter tells his readers that "Christ died for sins once for all, the righteous for the unrighteous, to bring you to God" (1 Pet 3:18).

John the Baptist called Jesus the spotless Lamb which God had provided for the sacrifice which would take away the world's sin (Jn 1:29). Because of that sacrifice, God can now forgive sins. The price for sin has been fully paid, once for all, by Jesus.

Redemption

That price is often referred to as a ransom—a price paid in ancient times to set a prisoner free. Later on the word ransom came to be used for the price paid for a slave to gain his freedom and, among the Jews, for the price a man could pay to redeem his life. For example, Exodus 21:28–31 lays down that if a man's bull gored someone to death, the owner could be liable to be put to death with the bull, because he had not kept the animal under control. However, the man could "redeem his life by paying what is demanded" (Ex 21:30).

This process is called *redemption* and is defined as "deliverance from some evil by the payment of a price."[29] The Bible tells us that we were all slaves to sin[30], under the just sentence of death,[31] spiritually bankrupt, without any hope of redeeming ourselves from the penalty of sin.[32] However, on Calvary, Jesus willingly gave his life to pay the ransom price God demanded to set us free. Jesus himself told us that he came "to give his life a ransom for many" (Mk 10:45).

Because of the Cross, we can be set free from the terrible bondage of sin and live as free men. However, we must remember that that freedom is given to us to serve God. When Paul talks about us being "bought with a price" (1 Cor 6:19f, 7:22f), and being "redeemed from the curse of the law" (Gal 3:13), by the death of Christ, he tells us that we are not set free in order to indulge in sin but rather to live to the glory of God.

To turn Christian forgiveness into a licence to sin is a terrible travesty of what Christianity is all about. Jesus, we are told, "loved righteousness and hated wickedness" (Heb 1:9). Therefore he gave his life so that men would be delivered from the wickedness he hated to the righteousness he loved. Because he paid the ransom, we are forever under obligation to him. As Paul tells the wayward Corinthians, "You are not your own; you

were bought with a price. Therefore honour God with
your body" (1 Cor 6:19–20).

Propitiation

We have already established the fact of the wrath of
God towards sinners. The "god" of easy morality who
will let sinners off like some understanding and benign
grandparent is nowhere found within the pages of the
Bible. Even when the Bible tells us that the Lord is
"slow to anger, and abounding in love," it adds the
solemn warning that "he does not leave the guilty
unpunished" (Num 14:18).

Of course, we must not look upon the wrath of God
like we do an outburst of human temper. His wrath has
its roots in his holiness, and it is complete and constant
displeasure with sin. Even we as sinners can experience
"righteous indignation" when we read of a little child
being raped and murdered or an old lady being conned
out of her life savings. Recently there was a public
outcry when a judge let a rapist off with a very light
sentence. Why? Because justice demands that a man
guilty of a horrible crime should be severely punished.

Therefore, to emphasise, as some do, the love of God
to the exclusion of everything else, is to accuse God of
moral flabbiness. His holiness and hatred of sin
demand that his wrath must strike the sinner—or a
lawful substitute. Only then will divine justice be satis-
fied. To expect anything less is to make God an
unrighteous judge.

To describe the work of the Cross in appeasing the
wrath of God the New Testament uses the word *propitiation*. Unfortunately, modern translators, wary of a word
which contains the idea of the wrath of God, have

tended to compromise by using words like "expiation" (RSV, NEB), and even the evangelical New International Version (NIV) translates the word "atoning sacrifice." However, as Leon Morris has shown in his scholarly book, *The Apostolic Preaching of the Cross*,[33] the Authorised Version was correct in translating the word propitiation.

Propitiation signifies the removal of wrath by the offering of a gift. Romans 3:25 and 1 John 2:2 & 4:10 describe Jesus as the propitiation for our sins; he died on the cross so that the wrath of God towards sinners might be appeased. Jesus gave himself as our lawful substitute, and at Calvary the wrath of God for our sin fell upon him rather than us. This is totally consistent with what Isaiah prophesied: "the Lord has laid on him the iniquity of us all" (Is 53:6). The prophet goes on to say these remarkable words about God's "Suffering Servant": "He was cut off from the land of the living for the transgression of my people, *to whom the blow was due*" (Is 53:8, margin).

Jesus, therefore, suffered the "blow" from the wrath of God that our sins deserved. The word "propitiation" vividly describes the death of Christ meeting the demands of God's holiness and hatred of sin and also his love of sinners.

However, Calvary must not be viewed as "the loving son appeasing the stern father." Some of our old hymns come very close to doing this and it is a misrepresentation of New Testament teaching. The fact is that propitiation has its origins in the love of God. Paul tells us that "*God presented him* [Jesus] as a propitiation" (Rom 3:25, my translation), and John is even more vivid in using the word to define the incredible love of God towards ungrateful, sinful man: "Herein is love, not that we loved God, but that he loved us, and sent his Son to be the propitiation for our sins" (1 Jn 4:10, KJV).

Calvary did not change God's attitude towards sinners—he has always loved them. But it enabled him righteously to change his *treatment* of them. Because of Christ's death as a substitute for sinners, God may now righteously forgive all those who will believe; God and sinful man may now be brought back together.

Reconciliation

This process of bringing God and man back together is called *reconciliation*. It is a word used for the making up after a quarrel. Two parties which were once at odds are now brought back together again; hostility is replaced by friendship. Of course, in order to reconcile the two parties we must deal with the cause of the quarrel; otherwise we shall merely have an easy peace, a "ceasefire" which may soon be broken.

The cause of our separation from God is sin. However, sin has not just caused a breakdown in relations; it is far more serious. The Bible bluntly calls sinners the "enemies" of God.[34] An enemy is not just someone who is not friendly; he is completely hostile and in the opposite camp!

We have seen already that God is hostile to all forms of sin, although he loves sinners. However, sinners, by their nature, are not just alienated from God, but "enemies" in their minds because of their evil behaviour (Col 1:21). Man is not just indifferent to God; he positively hates the God of the Bible. We see this enmity towards God seen in the terrible persecution of Christians, from Jesus himself right down to the present day. In fact, it has been estimated that during the present century more Christians have been martyred for Christ than at any other time in history. The reason? Man's hatred of the true God. As Jesus told his disciples: "If the world hates you, keep in mind that it hated me first" (Jn 15:18).

In order that God and man would be brought back together again, the cause of their hostility, sin, had to be dealt with. When sin was put away by the death of Christ, the way was open for reconciliation. Colossians tells us that God's purpose was, through Christ, "to reconcile to himself all things," and that this has been accomplished "through his blood, shed on the cross" (Col 1:20). Jesus is described, therefore, as "making peace" (Col 1:20 and Eph 2:15). Through Calvary he becomes the one who reconciles man to God. It is man's responsibility, therefore, to accept the peace Jesus offers. Paul tells the Corinthians, "We implore you on Christ's behalf: be reconciled to God" (2 Cor 5:20).

And man's reconciliation to God has an important side effect: that of reconciling man with his fellow man. Paul was only too aware in the ancient world, of the divisions that existed between men, the chief of which was the hostility between Jew and Gentile, which he describes in Ephesians 2:11f.

Similarly today, we see the catastrophic divisions in our modern world: quarrelling between neighbours, fighting between different ethnic groups, or full-scale war between nations, all testify to man's inability to live in harmony with his fellow human beings. Hatred and suspicion are seen, not only between nations, but between the differing races, classes and age groups in our society. Add to that the dreadful loneliness and alienation which have become an integral part of our modern Western civilisation, fuelling the suicide rate, and we see that in addition to separating man from God, sin has also permanently fractured his relationships with his fellow man.

The wonderful "spin-off" from man being reconciled to God, is that he is also enabled to live with his fellow man—not just to put up with him, but to love him as his brother. Paul, writing to Gentile Christians in Ephesus and the surrounding area, tells them that both Jew and Gentile are both reconciled to God through the work of Christ on the cross, "by which he put to death their hostility" (Eph 2:16). The impassable gap between Jew and Gentile was bridged; through Christ they had become brothers. This truth applies for all who believe. All divisions of race, class and gender are bridged when men come to Christ: "There is neither Jew nor Greek, slave nor free, male or female, for you are all one in Christ Jesus" (Gal 3:28).

Because of Christ, men who are reconciled to God can live together as brothers, part of the body of Christ. Hate and suspicion might be the norm for the world, but for those in the Church, love has taken their place. In fact, love for other Christians is one of the "acid tests" of our truly being reconciled to God. As John tells us: "We know that we have passed from death to life, because we love our brothers" (1 Jn 3:14). The answer, then, to the strife and hatred in the world does not lie in legislation and peace treaties, but in reconciling men to God through the Gospel of Jesus Christ.

4

Justification by Faith

Imagine yourself in court, in the "dock", and facing a serious charge. The evidence has been heard and the jury are filing back after considering their verdict. You are told to stand, which you do with heart thumping in your chest. "Gentlemen of the jury," says the judge, "how find you the prisoner—guilty or not guilty?" To your great relief the foreman calls out, "Not guilty, your honour." "Therefore," says the judge, "you may leave the court without a stain on your character."

If to stand before an earthly court is an unnerving experience, how much more awesome will it be to have to stand before God on the day when he judges all men![35] What will be his verdict on us? Will we be able to enter heaven without a stain on our character? Or will we be condemned to an eternity of torment, shut away from the presence of God?

The basic question which lies at the root of all religion is this: How are sinful people to be justified before a holy God? The word "justify", as found in the Bible, is a legal term meaning "to acquit, to reckon, or declare or show to be righteous"; ie to declare "not guilty". It does not mean "to make righteous"; justification has to do with our legal state, not our actual state.

The value of any religion is how it deals with the question of how man is justified in the sight of God, and Christianity is unique among the religions of the world in telling us that the justification of sinners is entirely the work of God, accomplished through Christ at Calvary. Through his work alone a guilty sinner, on believing, is declared "not guilty".

The Verdict

The Bible emphatically says that a man will never be justified by anything that he does. Neither his own morality nor his attempts to observe the law of God (summed up by the 10 commandments[36]) will justify him. "Therefore," says Paul, invoking the image of the law court, "no-one will be declared righteous [justified] in his [God's] sight by observing the law [of God]" (Rom 3:20).

Why is this? The problem, as we have seen, is sin. Sin means that man is unable to keep the law at every point as God demands. We do not have to think very far back in an average week to find we have all failed to keep the 10 commandments in many points.[37] Even in an earthly court, breaking the law at even one point puts us under condemnation to the law of the land. For example, if you are found guilty of stealing, it is no good pleading your cause by telling the judge at least you didn't murder someone! You are guilty and under condemnation by breaking just that one part of the law.

Justification by trying our best to keep the law of God is therefore impossible. In fact, Paul says, our natures are so perverse, that the law actually *awakens* sinful desires in us.[38] Therefore, however much I struggle to obey, however much my mind desires to obey God's law, my nature will not allow me to do it.

I have always had a passion for cricket; unfortunately, I have never been any good at the game. I seem to lack co-ordination between hand and eye so that I can hardly see the ball, let alone hit it! However good my intentions, however much I study a coaching manual, my basic lack of co-ordination will always keep me from succeeding. In fact, the more I try, the worse I get! Paul tells us we are like that with God's law: however good our intentions, however great our Bible knowledge and religious observances, "what I do is not the good I want to do; no, the evil I do not want to do—that I keep doing" (Rom 7:19).

Why, then, did God give the law? Certainly not to justify men. "Rather, through the law, we become conscious of sin" (Rom 3:20). The law is like a plumb-line or a spirit level. It does not make the wall straight but tells us it is out of true. Similarly God's law condemns us all as sinners and tells us we cannot possibly justify ourselves. It tells us that "all have sinned and fall short of the glory of God" (Rom 3:23), so that we, realising the helplessness and hopelessness of our plight, may turn to God and be "justified freely through the redemption that came by Christ Jesus" (Rom 3:24).

A Free Gift

The wonderful good news ("Gospel") of Christianity is that God, through the cross of Christ, has done everything necessary to justify us. We have seen that our sins were laid on Christ at Calvary, that the punishment for sin was fully carried by him. He has paid the full price and penalty for sin. Therefore, through the blood of Christ, shed on the cross, we can be justified, declared "not guilty" in the heavenly court, and saved from God's wrath.[39] All we have to do in order to be saved is to accept the free gift God he offers in Christ—that gift is eternal life.

Faith

Does this mean, then, that all men are automatically justified before God? The Bible knows of no such form of "universalism". According to the New Testament, justification is given when people believe in the Lord Jesus Christ. Paul tells the Jews in Pisidian Antioch, "Through him everyone who believes is justified" (Acts 13:39).

Later, the apostle gives the classic exposition of the theme in the book of Romans. Romans chapters 1—8 has one theme: the way to peace with God is justification by faith (Rom 5:1). By faith, Paul teaches, we are justified apart from anything we do (Rom 3:28). When we believe, a wonderful transaction takes place: our sins are taken and laid on Christ, and Christ's righteousness is given us (Rom 3:22). Therefore, we can stand before God, clothed in· Christ's righteousness, with our sin having been taken away. God's verdict: "Not guilty!" Though we are, in reality sinners, through faith in the work of Christ we have been declared righteous. "Therefore, there is now no condemnation for those who are in Christ Jesus" (Rom 8:1).

However, we must be careful to define what faith actually is. Every pastor has experienced the sorrow of seeing people profess to believe in Christ, but after a time lapse into a superficial "once on Sunday" Christianity or even fall away altogether. What had happened to them? Were they really saved in the first place?

The answer is that the faith that leads to justification

is "from the heart" (Rom 10:9–10); it is not mere intellectual belief, or even being moved upon by the emotion of a meeting. To the writers of the New Testament, the heart was not merely the seat of the emotions; to believe "with the heart" meant believing with the whole person. True faith, therefore, involves a complete surrender of the thoughts, the feelings and the will to Christ; it is a conviction that governs the whole inner being and consequently shapes a person's outward life.

Therefore, true saving faith will always lead to actions. James tells us that faith that is not accompanied by deeds is not true saving faith (Jas 2:14) because "Faith without deeds is dead" (Jas 2:26). These deeds do not, of course, do not make us acceptable to God; but they are an evidence that God has accepted us!

Jesus himself taught that, "Not everyone who says to me, 'Lord, Lord,' will enter the kingdom of heaven, but only he who does the will of my Father who is in heaven" (Mt 7:21). He told his disciples that, if they loved him, they would obey his commands (Jn 14:15). Paul himself, at the end of the great thesis on justification by faith, tells his readers to present their bodies as "living sacrifices" (Rom 12:1). For, as R. A. Torrey has said, "We are justified by faith alone, but we are justified by that faith alone that works."[40]

5

God's Sons

Wonderful though the thought of justification is, we must go on to realize fully all the benefits that come to us from it. The tragedy of many Christians is that they simply view themselves as forgiven sinners; they will get to heaven, but very little else.

For God's purpose for man goes far beyond mere forgiveness of sins, wonderful though that is. God's purpose for us is to share the glory of his Son in heaven; and in order that this might happen he has adopted us into his family.[41] Therefore, the wonderful position of the believer is that he is not merely a servant of God— he is a son. And being a son, he is always assured of a very special place in God's affection. For if God's Old Testament people were the "apple of his eye",[42] how much closer are God's ties to those he now calls his sons!

Romans 8:28–39 climaxes Paul's great thesis on justification, as he outlines God's plan for his people. The trials here on earth are merely a preparation for God's main purpose for us—glory. Is God the mean, miserly figure he is so often portrayed as? Never! Rather, "He who did not spare his own Son, but gave him up for us all—how will he also, along with him, graciously give us all things?" (v 32). Will anything come that will condemn us in the sight of God? How can it, since it is "God who justifies" (v 33). Can it be, even in our

41

darkest moments of despair on this earth, that something will come between us and God? Paul is adamant: "I am convinced that neither death nor life, neither angels nor demons, neither the present nor the future, nor any powers, neither height nor depth, nor anything else in all creation, will be able to separate us from the love of God that is in Christ Jesus our Lord" (vv 38–39).

This is God's wonderful purpose for the Christian; and it is all made possible by the work of Jesus on the cross. But how do we know that the cross has done all these things? How do we know that the death of Jesus really did take away sin? God provided the answer in a single historical act: he raised Jesus from the dead. Jesus was "delivered over to death for our sins and was raised to life for our justification" (Rom 4:25).

And it is to the events of the third day which we shall now turn.

Notes for Part 1

1. Mt 27:33
2. Mk 15:26. A placard stating the charge against condemned man was hung round his neck as he was led to the place of execution. The charge was then nailed above his head when he was crucified.
3. Lk 23:34
4. Jn 19:30
5. Lk 23:45
6. 1 Pet 1:20; Rev 13:8
7. Lk 24:25–27; 1 Pet 1:10–11
8. Lk 9:28–36
9. 2 Kings 20:3
10. Jn 12:32
11. 1 Cor 2:2
12. 1 Cor 1:22–24

13. John Bunyan, *Pilgrim's Progress*
14. Gen 1:26–30
15. Jn 15:18–25
16. Hab 1:13
17. Lk 12:5
18. Jn 3:18
19. Rev 20:11–15
20. Gen 3:15
21. Jn 1:14
22. D. Martyn Lloyd-Jones, *God's Ultimate Purpose* (Banner of Truth), p 166.
23. Lk 23:13–16
24. Mt 17:2
25. L. Morris, *The Atonement* (IVP), p 12.
26. Gen 2:17; Rom 6:23
27. Gen 4:3–4
28. See the book of Leviticus
29. *Illustrated Bible Dictionary* (IVP), p 1321
30. Jn 8:34
31. Rom 6:23
32. Eph 2:12
33. L. Morris, *The Apostolic Preaching of the Cross* (Tyndale Press).
34. eg Rom 5:10; Col 1:21; Jas 4:4
35. See Rev 20:11–15
36. Ex 20:1–17
37. Jas 3:2
38. Rom 7:7–12
39. Rom 5:9
40. R. A. Torrey, *What the Bible Teaches* (Revell), p 319.
41. Jn 1:12–13; Rom 8:14
42. Zech 2:8

Part 2

Sunday Comes...
Death Is Conquered!

Part 2

INTRODUCTION

The young Jewish woman stood peering into the rock-hewn tomb, typical of the many hundreds of such places of burial around Jerusalem. But this one was different—it had, to her mind, been desecrated. The body of the young prophet of Galilee was missing. Not content with crucifying him on a trumped-up charge, the authorities had now subjected his body to the ultimate indignity, denying him even in death the dignity of burial, and denying those who loved him the opportunity of anointing his body according to custom.

As she stood there, the sobs of grief heaving in her breast, she heard a movement behind her, and a gentle voice, "Woman, why are you crying?" Blinded by her tears and with sorrow numbing her mind, she supposed the voice to come from the gardener. She asked for any information he might have on the night's clandestine activities, particularly as to where her Lord's body was. Then at least she might retrieve the body from the place where it had no doubt been unceremoniously disposed of and give it a decent re-burial.

Then the voice which she loved more than anything on earth spoke one word, her name, "Mary", in such a personal and unmistakable way that in an instant the sorrow and despair were swallowed in a vibrant expression of faith and love: "O my Master!" she exclaimed, and clung to him. Her joy and enthusiasm at seeing him were so great that even her risen Lord had to gently check her! Awe-struck yet filled with inexpressible joy, the formerly notorious woman, Mary of Magdala, rushed back to the unbelieving disciples of Jesus and burst in on them with the news which has thrilled the hearts of Christians for centuries, "I have seen the Lord."[1]

Nor was her testimony left unsupported for long. Within a short period of time, those same disciples who had looked upon Mary's story as an idle tale of a hysterical woman were brought up sharp when none other than their leader, Simon Peter, came in with shining face also claiming to have seen Jesus alive. Unbelief was now giving way to optimistic and joyful hope, so that when two exhausted travellers, who had earlier left for Emmaus, burst in telling of their incredible experience of Jesus breaking bread with them, the disciples could only exclaim, "The Lord has indeed risen."[2]

Then came the moment they had waited for, yet dreaded with the fear of all men unacquainted with the supernatural. Though doors and windows were tightly barred Jesus himself stood in the middle of the room. As he showed them his hands and his feet, still bearing the marks cruelly made by the nails, fear was replaced by an overwhelming joy.[3] Jesus had risen from the dead! All that the prophets had spoken about him was true. He was without doubt the long awaited Messiah, the Son of the living God. A new era, they sensed, was beginning.

Within a few weeks, those same disciples who had ignominiously fled in terror on the night of Jesus' arrest were boldly standing in defiance of the Jewish authorities proclaiming, "This Jesus whom you crucified,

God has raised from the dead. We are witnesses to this." So convincing were they in their testimony that 3000 people on the first day alone believed them to become followers of the crucified Jesus of Nazareth.[4]

Cornerstone

The resurrection of Christ is the cornerstone of the Christian faith. Disprove it, says the apostle Paul, and the whole of our faith is in vain. However, to hear some modern churchmen talk, it would appear an irrelevance whether Jesus rose or not. After all, they say, in this scientific age we cannot possibly expect people to believe in a supernatural event such as a literal resurrection. What is therefore needed is is for people to have an "Easter experience", a "spiritual resurrection". Like John Brown it does not matter whether Jesus' body lies mouldering in the grave, as long as his "spirit" goes marching on in the teaching and example of those who in some way follow him.

Such theorising is as far removed from the vibrant faith of the early church as it is possible to be. The very term, "resurrection", gives lie to certain current theories that even the Gospel writers themselves did not believe in a literal resurrection. As F. F. Bruce says, "By 'resurrection' they (the early disciples) meant the resurrection of the body; if they had meant only that the spirit and power of Jesus lived on, 'resurrection' is not the word they would have used."[5]

Certainly the converted pharisee, Paul of Tarsus, would have denounced modern attempts to discredit the resurrection just as surely as he did in his great resurrection chapter, 1 Corinthians 15. In this chapter, written less than thirty years after the event, the apostle tells us that the early church held it to be "of first importance: that Christ died for our sins according to the Scriptures, that he was buried, that he was raised on the third day according to the Scriptures" (1 Cor 15:3–4). Hence Paul calls upon early church tradition backed up by the witness of the early disciples and Old Testament prophecy to substantiate his case.

In fact, Paul goes so far as to tell us that "if Christ has not been raised, your faith is futile" (1 Cor 15:17). He, along with the rest of the New Testament writers held the supreme importance of believing in a literal, physical resurrection of Jesus from the dead. What's more, they could produce plenty of evidence to support this claim.

6

The Evidence

Any Objections?

To all who approach the subject in an open-minded manner, the historical evidence for this world-shaking event is overwhelming. However, there are those today, as in the time of the early church, who treat the whole thing with scepticism and do their best to disprove it. For the sake of clarity we shall list the main objections to the resurrection before presenting the evidence:

(i) the whole notion of a resurrection is unscientific, for modern science has proved that dead men do not rise again.

(ii) the New Testament documents are unreliable romances, put about by members of Jesus' followers in order to keep the movement alive after Jesus' death.

(iii) Jesus did not really die on the cross; he actually only swooned and was mistakenly taken down before death had taken place. The cold of the tomb in which he was laid brought him round. He was therefore able to leave the tomb empty and convince his disciples that he was alive and raised from the dead.

(iv) the disciples went to the wrong tomb, very like the one which Jesus was laid in. Finding it empty, they naturally assumed that he was risen.

(v) the disciples stole the body of Jesus when the guards were asleep, and then proceeded to invent the story of the resurrection.

(vi) the disciples were hallucinated or victims of wishful thinking. The only way they saw Jesus "risen" was in their mind's eye or in the form of some sort of vision.

The Appliance of Science?

Is the resurrection "unscientific"? There are those who would say that Jesus' life and teaching are the important things about our faith—the resurrection merely adds a supernatural irrelevance which modern, scientific man finds impossible to believe. This, of course, is nothing new. Mankind in general has always found the resurrection a stumbling block; but, then, these same people also stumble over the whole doctrine of a crucified Christ. From the first Easter day men have found it more comfortable to mind and conscience to dismiss the resurrection. Hence the incredulity of the Jewish authorities in Jerusalem[6] on the first Easter day, followed much later by equal disbelief from many of the sceptical Athenian philosophers who heard Paul's sermon on Mars Hill. It is significant that, as soon as he mentioned the resurrection, "some mocked."[7] After all, to their enlightened, "scientific" minds, such an event was impossible.

The problem with the so-called "scientific" approach is that it is not really scientific at all. To try to argue "scientifically" that the resurrection could not happen because such an occurrence cannot be proved by the laws of science, is to misuse science. Science deals with observations of repeatable, natural occurrences, like measuring the movement of a stone falling to earth, as Newton did when formulating the laws of gravitation. However, science cannot be used to analyse unique, supernatural events like the resurrection. They are simply beyond the realm of the natural scientist.

Nor are the "laws" of science anything more than observations; apples were falling to earth long before "Newton's Law" was formulated! God is the author and sustainer of the laws of nature, and therefore he is certainly not bound by them. To say that it is "scientifically impossible" for God to raise Jesus from the dead is to try to contain God within the same limitations as ourselves.

Take it to Court!

A more appropriate approach for discussing the resurrection is that used in a court of law, where a case is proved or disproved by the reliability of witnesses or documents. That a story may seem incredible to us does not necessarily rule it out if reliable witnesses can be found to attest it. For example, anyone reading an account of the rescue of Israeli hostages from the Entebbe airport, Uganda, in 1976 may be forgiven for thinking that the whole story was the fabrication of a Hollywood scriptwriter in his wilder moments! However, the historical fact of the Entebbe raid could be easily proved by interviewing those who were involved at the time, and also by reading the contemporary accounts that were written.[8]

A similar approach can be used for examining the evidence for the resurrection. The early witnesses are found in the gospel narratives and the fifteenth chapter of Paul's first letter to the Corinthian Church. When you read the accounts of Jesus' resurrection appearances in the gospel narratives, they bear striking indications of being eye-witness accounts. The stories

are narrated with an artless simplicity, characterised by
the unspectacular straightforwardness of men who do
not need to resort to exaggeration in order to be
believed. As we read the accounts our immediate reac-
tion is, "This man is telling the truth."

To this must be added the fact that pious Jews of
Jesus' day had a great regard for the truth; their Law
dictated that any case could only be proved "in the
mouth of two witnesses." This is seen in the trial of
Jesus himself when certain false witnesses accused
Jesus; even the hostile high priests had to dismiss the
evidence when the witnesses did not agree (see Mk
14:59). It is therefore extremely unlikely that the early
followers of Christ deliberately indulged in concocting a
falsehood, and this is also seen in the fact that almost all
of them laid down their lives rather than deny the
resurrection. Surely men are not prepared to die for
something they know to be false from the beginning.

It must be admitted that some have used the differences in the four evangelists' accounts of the resurrection appearances as a case against the historical
accuracy of the gospel record. The different accounts,
they say, contradict one another and and cannot be
reconciled. However, differences are not necessarily
contradictions, and although there are difficulties in
fitting the gospel accounts together into one story, their
very differences do bear record that the evangelists were
writing independently of each other. Nowhere do the
writers give the impression of having carefully collabo-
rated in order to propagate a story they knew to be
untrue. Added to which, the distinguished New Testament scholar, John Wenham, has recently shown that,
by making a few reasonable assumptions, it is quite
possible to harmonize the Gospel accounts without any

distortion of the text.[9] We shall look at this later, but first let us see the main historical evidence for believing Jesus rose from the dead.

(i) *Jesus died and was buried* (1 Cor 15:3–4). The execution of Jesus was carried out by Roman soldiers who knew their business and who were likely to forfeit their lives if they failed in their duty. Death by crucifixion was long and painful, but could be hastened by the barbarous practice of shattering the legs with a mallet. This is what happened to the thieves crucified with Jesus at the request of the Jewish authorities (Jn 19:31), so that the bodies would not defile the coming Passover. However, when the soldiers came to Jesus they recognised that his death had been unusually swift in coming, a fact which surprised Pilate. This has led to the speculation that Jesus did not really die but only swooned on the cross. He later revived in the tomb, moved the stone, and walked out on wounded feet to convince his disciples he had risen from the dead!

This unlikely theory, however, is completely scuppered by John recording that, in order to make sure Jesus was dead, one of the soldiers thrust a spear into his side, under the rib cage and into the distended heart, bringing a flow of "blood and water" (Jn 19:34). Whatever the medical explanation for this (Jesus' heart may have ruptured?) it is clear that the body was lifeless when it was taken from the cross. The only way Jesus could have appeared to his disciples is by rising from the dead.

(ii) *On the third day, the tomb in which Jesus was laid was discovered empty.* The bodies of crucified victims were left to rot and be eaten by carrion unless a relative or friend was around to bury them. Hearing Jesus was dead, Joseph of Arimathea, a wealthy Jew and a secret disciple of Jesus, came to the fore. Having failed to acknowledge the young prophet during his life, Joseph determined in some way to make amends by giving the body a decent burial. Boldly going to Pilate, he asked for Jesus' body and the governor granted his request. Joseph and another secret disciple, Nicodemus, carried the body to a tomb Joseph had hewn for himself. They hastily wrapped the body in a linen sheet, together with a fabulous offering of spices provided by Nicodemus, and rolled a stone across the entrance.[10]

Alarmed by such proceedings, and fearful of Jesus' words that he would rise on the third day, the Jewish authorities asked Pilate for a guard for the tomb, in case the disciples should steal the body and continue to propagate the fraud. With Pilate's permission, the tomb was guarded (with a platoon of up to sixteen soldiers) and a seal placed on it. The seal was an official warning to thieves or vandals that the site should not be disturbed on pain of Imperial displeasure. Yet in spite of all these precautions, the stone was rolled away and the body gone.[11]

Could the disciples have stolen it while the guards slept? This is the story that the incredulous Jewish authorities put out; but it is unlikely that even they themselves believed it. The punishment for a guard sleeping on duty was severe, and in any case it is unlikely that all of them would have slept together; and how did the disciples manage to move that huge stone without waking anyone up?

The simple fact behind this story is that such was the unbelief and cynicism of the chief priests that even investigation of the story told by the terrified guards was out of the question. After all, like some professional churchmen of today, the Jewish leaders treated tales of supernatural activity with disbelief. Therefore the only recourse they had was to lies. Taking advantage of the fact that the guards had already committed a serious breach of military discipline by leaving the tomb, they found it easy, with the aid of a bribe, to persuade the soldiers to put about the story that Matthew recounts in Mt 28:12–15.

It is sometimes speculated that the disciples were mistaken and went to the wrong tomb. Hence the empty tomb they found was not the guarded tomb of Jesus but one very similar to it, which happened to be empty. This is, of course, possible except for one vital thing: why, when news of the resurrection was spreading like wildfire in Jerusalem, did the authorities not simply produce the body of Jesus from the real tomb? The answer is, of course, that there was no body to produce. No mistake was made—Jesus' tomb was really empty.

(iii) *There was a tremendous change in the disciples*. The Bible is not kind to its heroes. It paints them "warts and all." On the night of Jesus' arrest, those who boasted they would die with him took to their heels and fled.[12] Peter, in a fit of panic, even denied knowing Jesus with curses and oaths.[13] Only the faithful John and some women were with the Lord in his sufferings.[14] Over that weekend there was settled upon those disciples a spirit of fear, mixed with shame and hopelessness. Behind locked doors they planned how they could escape from Jerusalem after the festival.[15]

Yet within a few weeks those same men were proclaiming the message of Jesus with such conviction that thousands believed them and joined the young Church. Fear and unbelief had been replaced by vibrant faith and certainty. Read the early sermons in the Acts of the Apostles and you will find an authority, a certainty and a fearless courage in the face of all sorts of threats and beatings. Something stupendous had certainly happened to change the lives of those Galillean fishermen.[16] The explanation is that they really believed that they had seen Jesus alive! The fact that the resurrection played such a part in the preaching of the early church can leave us in no doubt that the apostles not only believed it themselves, but also believed that it could not be disproved by the authorities.

Outside Evidence

Two testimonies outside the immediate band of disciples are worth noting. James, the step-brother of Jesus, together with the rest of his family, was a rank unbeliever during Jesus' life[17]. However, after Jesus' death we find that he, along with the rest of his brothers, is a disciple[18]. James later became the leader of the Jerusalem church, finally suffering martyrdom for the Christian faith. The only plausible explanation for this change is the one given in 1 Corinthians 15:7, "He [Jesus] appeared to James."

A few years later a young Jewish zealot, Saul of Tarsus, was leading a fanatical persecution of the Jesus sect. Setting off for Damascus, the young pharisee vowed to root out any Nazarene heretics there and bring them to justice. This cult that was polluting the pure religion of his fathers must be stopped at all cost! Yet on his arrival at Damascus Saul is changed beyond all recognition. He now preaches the faith he once

attempted to destroy—preaching with such fervour
and conviction that his former friends try to kill him![19]
But he escapes and becomes Paul, the mighty apostle to
the Gentiles, perhaps the greatest Christian leader of all
time. What caused the change? Again, the only explanation worth consideration is that given by Paul himself:
"Last of all he (Jesus) appeared to me." (1 Cor 15:8)

All in the mind?

Is it possible that all these disciples could have been
mistaken, or hallucinated, or that they simply held
strong yet fanciful convictions? Perhaps if we had only
the testimony of Mary of Magdala, we would wonder
whether it might have been the illusion of a hysterical
and distraught woman. But would men like blustering
Peter, doubting Thomas and intellectual Paul be so
misled? None of these men were expecting to see Jesus
when he first appeared to them, and that goes for the
rest of the disciples, so theories of hallucination and
wishful thinking just do not fit in. It seems that there
may have been more of an air of expectancy later on,
but would all of the 500 people who, according to an
open letter of Paul (1 Cor 15:6), saw Jesus at once, have
hallucinated or been deceived? The letter was written
less than thirty years after the resurrection, so there
were, as Paul remarks, plenty of them still left alive to
bear witness to what they saw.

Some critics, scraping the barrel of scepticism to its
limit, have propagated the pathetic notion that Saul of
Tarsus was epileptic and it was an epileptic fit that
changed his life on the road to Damascus. I have known
many people with this unfortunate complaint, and I

have yet to see such a life-changing experience result from it!

One Conclusion

In fact, when we look at the evidence for the resurrection fairly, there can be only one conclusion, as there was for the one time sceptical lawyer, Frank Morison. Brought up in a rationalistic environment, Morison decided to write an account of the last days of Jesus, whom he admired as one of the world's unjustly martyred heroes. However, he would utterly discount the resurrection, which he considered to be nothing but a fairy-tale ending which spoiled the matchless story of Jesus. However, after a thorough but fair investigation into the resurrection accounts Morison had to conclude that, "there certainly is a deep and profound historical basis for that much disputed sentence in the Apostles' Creed, 'The third day He rose again from the dead.' "[20] The original book, in Morison's own words, "refused to be written." The volume that he did write, *Who moved the Stone?*, became a best-seller and remains one of the shrewdest and most convincing proofs of the resurrection one can read.

In the light of this, we may suspect that the real reason for man's disbelief in the resurrection of Jesus throughout the centuries is not that the stories are incredible. After all, if we do believe in an all-powerful God, we may say, as Paul did to Agrippa, "Why should you consider it incredible that God raises the dead?" (Acts 26:8) Rather, modern man "loves darkness rather than light because his deeds are evil" (Jn 3:19). Hence he erects a pseudo-scientific, intellectual facade to hide behind. It is amazing that people will accept Caesar's accounts of the Gallic wars without blinking an eye, but treat the far better attested facts of the resurrection with incredulity. The reason is not the evidence; it is the challenge and responsibility that a risen Christ brings to a man.

7

The Appearances of Jesus

What of the varying accounts of the resurrection? Is it possible to make sense of them, or are they, as some would say, hopelessly contradictory? The first thing is to note that they are obviously accounts from different sources that the evangelists have used. We need to remember that we are dealing with various descriptions of an event as seen through the eyes of independent witnesses; we are not dealing with statements made under cross-examination. Even today, with high technology reporting, one may read two differing newspaper accounts of, say, a football match, and wonder whether the two reporters were at the same game! It is not, however, that either reporter is inaccurate or dishonest, but that they have seen the game from different angles. Hence differences in the gospel accounts are not contradictions but the results of independent witnesses making differing observations. No doubt, if we had the witnesses still with us to cross-examine, many of our present difficulties would be cleared up immediately.

To this can be added the fact that the writers of New Testament days did not place such a high priority on detailed order of events as we do today. Hence we get Matthew's "telescoping" of events, for example, in his story of the women at the tomb. Throughout his gospel he often puts several hours' or even days' activity into a few verses.[21] This is not inaccuracy, but it means that

Matthew and the other evangelists had different priorities from those we expect today. Agreeing on the basic similarities of the narratives, we can build a provisional picture of the order of events on and after that first Easter Day.

Sunday Morning

Early on the Sunday morning a group of women were due to meet at the tomb of Jesus and finish the task of anointing the body with spices. They may have been unaware of the already substantial offering made by Nicodemus, or may simply have wished to pay their own personal respects to their dead Lord. Amid the horrors and heartbreak of the previous couple of days, they appear not to have thought about the matter of moving the huge stone from the entrance of the tomb. However, unknown to them, the job had already been done by a heavenly messenger! "An angel of the Lord came down from heaven and, going to the tomb, rolled back the stone and sat upon it" (Mt 28:2). It would seem that he sat on the stone to frighten the guards, who at first "became like dead men" (Mt 28:4) and later took to their heels and ran! The angel, according to Mark 16:5, then waited inside the tomb for the women so as to reduce their fear of supernatural beings. The fact that Luke 24:4 and John 20:12 tell us that there were two angels is no contradiction; it merely means that Mark was interested only in the spokesman.

Of course the angel did not remove the stone to let Jesus out, but rather to allow the disciples to see the tomb was empty. The body of the Lord was already gone by then. We must not think of Jesus' resurrection in the same way as the raising of, say, Lazarus,[22] and assume that Jesus would have sat up, yawned, and proceeded to take off his grave clothes! John's account[23] tells us that the linen strips in which Jesus' body had been wrapped were still lying there where the body had been. The cloth that had covered his head lay folded up by itself, separate from the linen strips. Therefore Jesus' body had supernaturally passed *through* the burial sheets. It was raised a real but *spiritual* body, capable of things that a natural body cannot do, like passing through a wall. If someone objects that this is scientifically impossible, then the answer again is that the laws of natural science simply do not apply to a spiritual being like Jesus had become!

When the women arrived at the tomb it was empty with the guards gone. Mary of Magdala immediately ran off to fetch Peter and John who were probably staying reasonably close by.[24] In the meantime the other women looked into the tomb and saw the angels who told them to tell the disciples that the Lord had risen and they must prepare to go to Galilee.[25] The women hurried off to tell their story to the main body of disciples who may have been staying outside Jerusalem at Bethany.[26]

After they had gone, Peter and John arrived at the tomb with Mary. Puzzled, they looked in and believed her story, but could not comprehend what it meant.[27] Leaving the tomb, they hurried to tell the other disciples the news, leaving Mary at the tomb, where soon after she was the first to see the risen Lord (Jn 20:16). Soon afterwards, Jesus met the other women on the way to Bethany (Mt 28:8–10), again telling them that the disciples must meet him in Galilee. It was probably the rank unbelief of the disciples at the women's story that caused Jesus to appear to them at Jerusalem.

Then came the meeting with Cleopas and his friend on the Emmaus Road (Mk 16:12 and Lk 24:13–31); these two immediately ran back home, heedless of the dangers of night travelling, to be told that the Lord had appeared to Peter (Lk 24:34; 1 Cor 15:5). No sooner had they finished their story than Jesus appeared to all of them (Lk 24:36; Jn 20:19; 1 Cor 15:5). Thomas, of course was absent, and continued in his unbelief until the Lord's next appearance a week later (Jn 20:24–29). Then the disciples at last obeyed the Lord's instructions to go to Galilee.

When they arrived there, nothing happened for a while, so Peter decided to continue earning his living as a fisherman. After a night of much exertion for no result, they received instructions from a stranger by the lakeside. They not only caught a huge haul of fish but recognised that the stranger was the risen Lord himself (Jn 21). Typically, even in his risen state, the Lord was considerate enough to have a breakfast cooking for those hungry and tired fishermen!

It is probable that Jesus met many times with the disciples in Galilee, instructing them about the kingdom of God; Luke implies as much in Acts 1:3–5. At least one of these was an "arranged" meeting at which 500 Galillean disciples turned up and saw the risen Lord (1 Cor 15:6). This may have been the occasion when Jesus gave the "Great Commission" of Matthew 28:16–20. Some time in Galilee Jesus had a private meeting with James, his step-brother (1 Cor 15:7) and possibly others of his earthly family. The disciples then returned to Jerusalem as Jesus instructed them (Acts 13:31).

Back in Jerusalem came the final appearance (Acts 1:4) after which Jesus led his disciples to the Mount of Olives and ascended into heaven (Lk 24:50–53).

8

The Importance of The Resurrection

But, even given its historical basis, why the importance of the resurrection? Isn't it enough that we have the example and teaching of Jesus on record; and did not his great cry from the cross, "It is finished,"[28] mean that the work of redemption had been accomplished? Why did the preaching of the early church place so much emphasis on the events of the first Easter morning? The answer is that the resurrection has tremendous implications to the person and work of Jesus and to the whole subsequent future of the church.

(i) *The resurrection proves that the claims Jesus made for himself during his life are true.* During his ministry Jesus proclaimed himself as the Messiah, the bringer of good news, the fulfilment of all the prophets had spoken of. He accepted Peter's confession, "You are the Christ, the Son of the Living God"[29] to be true of himself. To the anger of the religious authorities he claimed to be Lord of the Sabbath[30] and added to their outrage by teaching that, "I and my Father are one."[31] He made an even more direct claim to deity by claiming to have the authority to forgive sins,[32] and on one occasion the Jews tried to stone him when he used the divine name of JAHWEH of himself in saying, "Before Abraham was, I AM."[33]

All of these claims were, of course, perfectly pre-

posterous, *unless they happened to be true!* By rising from
the dead, Jesus proved that all that he had taught about
himself was true. This is why a Jew like Paul, to whom
the thought of a crucified Messiah was sheer blas-
phemy, accepted Jesus' Messiahship *after he had met the
risen Lord.* It was the revelation of the crucified Jesus
risen from the dead that convinced Paul and all the other
disciples as well that Jesus was the Messiah, because he
was "declared with power to be the Son of God by his
resurrection from the dead" (Rom 1:4).

Without the resurrection, the whole of Jesus' teaching collapses like a pack of cards. If he was not raised,
then Jesus was an imposter, merely another in a long
line of Jewish fanatics of the day, albeit more ego-
centric and extreme in his claims than most. What's
more, his disciples were, at best, poor deceived fools or
else monumental liars! As Paul himself says, "if Christ
has not been raised,...we are then found to be false
witnesses about God, for we we have testified about
God that he raised Christ from the dead" (1 Cor 15:15).
In fact, without the resurrection, the name of Jesus of
Nazareth would have died with him at Calvary.

(ii) *The resurrection proves that Jesus' sacrificial death for sin
was accepted by the Father and that all who believe in Christ
will be justified before God.* Jesus defeated the sin principle
with his spotless life, but on Calvary he offered himself
in order to defeat sin and its power for every man. The
resurrection is the inevitable consequence of his tri-
umph, for in defeating sin Jesus also defeated the *consequences* of sin, the chief of which is death. However, if
death were able to hold Jesus, then it is proof that he
did not succeed, and that his sacrifice was not accepted
by the Father, for death (and therefore sin) would still

reign. Without the resurrection there is no atonement, and as Paul says, "if Christ has not been raised, your faith is futile and you are still in your sins" (1 Cor 15:17).

By raising Jesus from the dead, God declared that he accepted once and for all the settlement Christ made for sin on Calvary. Jesus was "delivered over to death for our sins and was raised to life for our justification" (Rom 4:25). Hence, when we put our faith in Jesus' sacrifice for sin, we are justified *(ie declared righteous)* before God. This is why the preaching of the apostles is so insistent on faith in a literal, physical resurrection of Christ as a condition of true Christian salvation. Paul lays down the conditions for true faith as follows: "if you confess with your mouth, 'Jesus is Lord,' and believe in your heart that God raised him from the dead, you will be saved" (Rom 10:9).

The implication of this is obvious: there is no true Christian faith outside of the risen Christ. All who seek to speculate about "spiritual" resurrections yet deny the literal resurrection of Christ, do not hold the same faith as the apostles; and who are we going to believe— our modern day sceptics or those who knew the Lord first hand, who saw him after he had risen and who finally laid down their lives for him? The "Jesus of faith" which certain liberal theologians appear so fond of talking about only has real meaning if we believe in the Jesus of history, the Son of God, risen from the dead. It is only though the life of the resurrected Christ that we can be saved.[34]

(iii) *The resurrection declares that Christianity is a vital, living, supernatural religion.* The Western culture today appears to be caught between two illogical extremes: a rejection of the supernatural content of the Christian faith (a view propagated, it must be admitted, by many who call themselves churchmen); and a seeking after God in areas like astrology, "New Age" religions, Eastern mysticism and even the occult. It is a tragic fact that many who pour scorn on the claims of Christianity are fascinated by psychics, T.M. gurus and avidly study their horoscopes in the paper; one of the reasons is that the church has failed to give them the hope of a living Christ.

Whatever good may or may not be found in other religions, they cannot offer anything to fallen humanity like the one who said, "I am the way, the truth and the life."[35] Because Christ is risen and is ascended at the right hand of God, then we can know a supernatural relationship with God when we put our faith and trust in him. This relationship comes through the Holy Spirit who the living Christ has given to all who obey him.[36] It has been the playing down of the miraculous content of the gospel that has robbed the Western world of hope; but the true apostolic preaching is of a risen Christ who is the way to God himself.

(iv) *The resurrection of Christ is the guarantee of our own resurrection.* The teaching of the New Testament is of a resurrection for all believers. We are not going to live in heaven as disembodied spirits, but one day be given new bodies just like Christ's resurrected body.[37] At the present time our service for God is limited because we still live in a body which has been ruined by the fall of man. One day, when Jesus comes again, we shall have a body like his with none of our present limitations.

How is this possible? That is the question Paul addresses in 1 Cor.15. Just as a fish has a body designed for the water and the bird for the air, so we will be given a body suitable for the spiritual realm of the new creation God will build after he has dispensed with the present, fallen one.[38] This spiritual body will know no sickness, pain or death—Christ has taken them all to his cross. Most wonderful of all, our resurrected body will be free from sin, capable of loving and serving God without hindrance. What a hope to look forward to! And it is not wishful "pie in the sky when you die"; because Christ is raised he has become "the firstfruits of those who have fallen asleep [ie died with faith in Christ]" (1 Cor 15:20). Therefore the Christian "hope" is more than just wishful thinking; it is a living certainty that "when he (Jesus) appears, we shall be like him, for we shall see him as he is" (1 Jn 3:2).

(v) *By the resurrection of Christ, God has given notice that there will be a day of judgment for all mankind*[39]. Jesus himself claimed that God would judge the world through him[40]; in that judgment men would be judged according to their acceptance or rejection of Jesus in this life. By raising Jesus from the dead, God has set his seal to that claim. The sure fact of Christ's resurrection in history points forward to the certainty of his judging the world in the future. Belief in a judgment day is not the speculation of theologians or the imaginings of religious extremists; it is a positive faith founded on a proven fact — the resurrection of Jesus Christ.

(vi) *Until the day we see Christ in his glory, we can, in this life, know the power of his resurrection.* Paul prays that he might know Christ and "the power of his resurrection" working in his life. He also prays that the Ephesian Christians may know (now) "his incomparably great power for us who believe." (Eph 1:19) That power is the same power that raised Christ from the dead, and which we receive into our lives when we are filled with the Holy Spirit. Paul talks about the Spirit as "the deposit guaranteeing our inheritance." (Eph 1:14) He is given as a foretaste and down payment of what is to come in order that we might know the power of the risen Christ working in us in this life. We are therefore able to be "more than conquerors"[41] in a world hostile to Christianity. Let us not live the Christian life on any level less than in the power of the risen Jesus! It is only by being joined to the risen Christ that our Christian lives can be fruitful.[42]

The Final Proof

This is, of course the final proof to us today that Jesus really is alive, that we know his life-changing power at work in us. Significantly, Luke begins the book of Acts by saying that in his first volume (ie the gospel of Luke) he "wrote about all Jesus *began* to do and to teach."[43] In other words, Jesus' ministry did not end with his ascension! He is still at work changing men and women today by the power of his resurrection. I can remember meeting a very old man in an old people's home I was visiting just after I had become a Christian. He was well over 90 years of age but his face shone with a radiance that was absent from the other faces in the home. The reason? He was quick to tell me: "I've walked with the Lord for seventy years, lad!" His body was ready for death, but he was already anticipating the glorious life that lay beyond the grave.

As a pastor, I have been privileged many times to observe the change Jesus can make in people's lives.

Many folk who, like those early disciples, were hopeless and despairing, have been radically changed by the new life Christ has given them. Here's just one example of what I mean: a mother of five children had suffered a nervous breakdown. Her life consisted of sitting in her room, smoking and suffering the effects of tranquilizers. The church I was pastoring contacted her through her children's attendance at Sunday school. One evening she came to a service at the church to see her daughter baptized. At the end of the meeting she went home and asked Jesus into her life. Within three months she was unrecognizable, having "kicked" the cigarettes and the tranquilizers. From being almost totally introverted, she became outgoing, and soon was a great visitor and a help to others. Later she took over the leadership, very successfully, of a group of girls in the church. What caused the transformation? None other than the power of the risen Christ working today in her life.

Since that first Easter day, countless millions of ordinary people have experienced that same power, and that is the final proof to us of what the historical facts so convincingly tell us: "The Lord is risen indeed."

Notes for Part 2

1. Jn 20:10–18
2. Lk 24:33–35
3. Lk 24:36f
4. Acts 2:41
5. F. F. Bruce, *The Real Jesus* (Hodder), p 117.
6. Mt 28:11–15
7. Acts 17:32
8. For a graphic account of this remarkable military operation see *Counterstrike Entebbe* by Tony Williamson (Collins).
9. See *Easter Enigma* by John Wenham (Paternoster Press).

10. Jn 19:38–42; Mt 27:57–61
11. Jn 20:1
12. Mk 14:50
13. Mk 14:66–72
14. Jn 19:25–27
15. Jn 20:19
16. Read the sermons in Acts 2:14–39; 3:11–26; and the defence before the Sanhedrin 4:8–20
17. Jn 7:5
18. Acts 1:14
19. Acts 9:19–25
20. F. Morison, *Who Moved the Stone?* (Faber), p 192.
21. For example, compare Matthew 21:1–22 with Mark 11:1–25. Whereas Mark gives his material in chronological order, Matthew presents the events separately. Mark is more concerned with a vivid narrative; Matthew wrote his gospel for teaching purposes. Both are valid approaches and are complementary rather than contradictory.
22. Jn 11:1–44
23. Jn 20:6–8
24. Jn 20:2
25. Mk 16:6–8
26. Mt 28:8
27. Jn 20:3–9
28. Jn 19:30
29. Mt 16:16
30. Mk 2:28
31. Jn 10:30
32. Mt 9:1–8
33. Jn 8:58
34. Rom 5:10
35. Jn 14:6
36. Acts 5:32
37. Phil 3:20–21
38. 1 Cor 15:35–56
39. Acts 17:31
40. Jn 5:22
41. Rom 8:37
42. Rom 7:4
43. Acts 1:1

Part 3

Today...Resurrection Life!

Part 3

INTRODUCTION

The famous evangelist climaxed his message, urging
people to come to Christ. After making his appeal, to
which many responded, he began giving the converts
instruction about beginning the Christian life. One of
the things he told them was to join a church. At this
point he became most apologetic! "Jesus went to the
'church' of his day even though it was corrupt, and he
expects us to do the same today."

What a tragedy that an evangelist should feel the
need to apologise for the greatest thing on earth—the
church of Jesus Christ. What a contradiction to his
message on how wonderful it was to be a Christian! But
an even greater tragedy that the church was in such a
state that he felt he needed to apologise for it! The late
David Watson once said that many people's attitude to
Christianity may be summed up as "Jesus—yes;
Church—no!"[1] I myself can remember being told:
"Don't look at the people in the church—look to
Christ!"

This view of the church as a weak, miserable bunch
of "Dad's Army Vicars" is in stark contrast to the New
Testament teaching of the Christian life. Jesus told his
disciples that they were to be the "salt of the earth" and
"the light of the world."[2] They were to so let their light
shine before men that people would see the quality of
their living and want to be like them.[3] This is not a call

to a "holy huddle"—or even to "hold the fort". Jesus did not see his people as a set of spiritual liabilities, forgiven but powerless. Rather, he said that he himself would build his church, and that church would be so mighty that even the gates of Hades itself would not be able to stand against it![4]

We see the early church fulfilling this task. Even though they were despised and often persecuted fiercely for their faith, so powerful was their living that they not merely survived, but changed the whole course of history. In spite of the fact that becoming a Christian often meant severe suffering, we are told that they "welcomed the message with the joy given by the Holy Spirit."[5] What's more, this same persecuted church was so vibrant that very soon it had become a witness to the far corners of the Roman Empire.

How did they do this? What is the secret of victorious Christian living? What makes us "more than conquerors"?[6] We often appear so weak and sinful beside the power of temptation and opposition in the world. Were the disciples in the early church "supermen"?

The answer is that they were people like us, just as prone to vacillation and failure. Peter was such a man, three times denying his Lord.[7] Even later in life he could still show the same tendency to weakness and compromise; so much so that Paul at one time had to take him publicly to task![8] What made Peter such a great servant of God did not lay in himself; rather in the knowledge of the power of the resurrected Christ within him. As an old man he tells his readers his secret: "[God's] divine power has given us everything we need for life and godliness through our knowledge of him who called us by his own glory and goodness" (2 Pet 1:3).

As God's children, we need to realise who we are in Christ and also just how great is God's power that lives in us. This realisation will enable us to live the sort of Christian life that will not only fill us with joy, but will also attract others to Christ. This is what Paul prayed for the Ephesians, that they would know God's "incomparably great power for us who believe" (Eph 1:19). He tells us that this power, available today for the ordinary Christian, "is like the working of his mighty strength, which he exerted in Christ when he raised him from the dead" (Eph 1:20). Hence, victorious Christian living does not depend on our own weak and feeble efforts; rather, realising the mighty power of the resurrected Christ which comes to dwell within us when we are "born again."

9

The New Birth

A New Creation

One church put a up a notice: "We Christians aren't any different—just forgiven!" Worthy though the motive was for the slogan, it shows a tragic misunderstanding of the teaching of the New Testament concerning what a Christian really is.

For, as we have seen already, salvation does not stop at mere forgiveness. We do not make a "decision" in an evangelistic meeting and then struggle unaided and most unsuccessfully with the Christian life until the wonderful day when we arrive in heaven!

Being a Christian involves a complete new life in Christ—a life of knowing God. This is often referred to as "eternal life", which Jesus defined in John 17:3 : "This is eternal life: that they know you, the only true God, and Jesus Christ, whom you have sent." To be a Christian is to know God! To know Jesus Christ! When we consider just who God is, to be a real Christian must be pretty exciting!

In order to enter this wonderful new life, Jesus tells us that we need to be "born again" (Jn 3:3). This is more than being religious, or even making a decision for Christ. It is nothing less than a complete, spiritual rebirth, which happens when we confess and turn from our sin and believe in the Lord Jesus Christ. When we do this the Holy Spirit makes us spiritually alive.

The great penalty man paid for sin was death; not just physical death, but spiritual death. He was cut off from God because sin had killed that part of him that could communicate with God. This is what Paul means when he tells the Ephesians they were "dead in transgressions and sins" (Eph 2:1). However, when the new birth takes place, God's Holy Spirit makes us "alive with Christ" (Eph 2:4). Because our sins are forgiven through the cross, God can now have a relationship with us; and to do so he makes our "God-sense" alive again.

This new birth, therefore, is far more than just turning over a new leaf or becoming religious. The Bible tells us that, "If anyone is in Christ, he is a new creation; the old has gone, the new has come" (2 Cor 5:17). As Christians, we certainly are, by the grace of God, different! We have become new creatures, capable of enjoying a relationship with God and, what's more, living a life in obedience to his commands.

Baptism

Everyone enjoys a baptismal service. The sight of new believers being immersed[9] always cheers the heart as it means that the church is succeeding in its witness. The children like the service because they want to see how many onlookers will be soaked if the pastor gets carried away! And for the new converts, there is the joy of the wonderful new life they have entered.

Baptism is more than just a sign of sins forgiven; it signifies just how radical a change has taken place within. When a believer is immersed, he is testifying that he is following Christ. And he begins by following him in death, burial and resurrection. We have already shown that Jesus died for sin, was buried and then raised on the third day. When a believer is baptised he is proclaiming publicly that he, too, has died to sin. He is now no longer the old, sinful man he was. Rather, he is a new man, living in the power of Christ's resurrection. Therefore he is "buried" in the water, then raised up again.

This is important, for it appears that many Christians do not realise the full significance of baptism. They look only on the burial; the fact the old man is "dead" and they will struggle to try and keep him lying down. However, this is far from the truth. I have conducted many baptismal services and I have never left anyone under the water yet!

Death without resurrection spells defeat not victory. We therefore need to realise that it is not just the old man who has died; we have been raised with Christ and made a new man: "having been buried with him in baptism and raised with him through your faith in the power of God, who raised him from the dead" (Col 2:12).

It is vital for us to realise that as we identify with Jesus' death and resurrection we shall be given victory over sin. Paul urges this upon his Roman readers: "Count yourselves dead to sin but alive to God in Christ Jesus" (Rom 6:11). In other words, realise what has happened to you! Through his death and resurrection, Jesus set you free from the power of sin and made you spiritually alive to serve God. Therefore, the apostle goes on, "Do not let sin reign in your mortal body so that you obey its evil desires" (Rom 6:12). Instead of offering our bodies to sin the way we used to, we are now set free by the power of the resurrected Christ. As he was brought from death to life by the power of God, so have we been.

This means, concludes Paul, that "sin shall not be your master, because you are not under law but under grace" (Rom 6:14). As Christians we are able to resist temptation and live lives in harmony with what God commands. We do not, of course, become sinless, because sin will always lurk in our bodies, ready to trip us up when we are off guard, till the day we die.

However, the only reason a Christian will live in defeat is because he does not realise that he is a free man. After the American Civil War all the slaves in the South were set free. However, many of them were so used to slavery, that they continued living as slaves although they were, in reality, free men. It is one of the greatest "con" tricks of the devil that he kids so many Christians they are still slaves to sin. However, as we realise what Christ has done and as we learn to share in his victory, we shall send the tempter packing.

10

A Great Helper

But how is this done? The good news is that God has not left us to live the Christian life unaided—that would be a sure recipe for disaster. Before he was crucified, Jesus told his disciples they would not be on their own: "I will not leave you as orphans; I will come to you" (Jn 14:18). A wonderful helper, the Holy Spirit, would be with them forever. In fact, Jesus said, "It is for your good that I am going away" (Jn 16:7).

Why was this seemingly tragic news going to be such a blessing to the disciples? Because Jesus, having conquered sin by his death and resurrection, ascended to heaven and, on the Day of Pentecost, poured out the Holy Spirit on the church.[10] The disciples were transformed from a weak and feeble bunch of fishermen to a mighty force which spread the Gospel of Jesus Christ throughout the known world.

The Holy Spirit is still just as active in the church today as he was in the beginning. His work in the Christian is best illustrated by the term Jesus uses for him in John's gospel ch. 14—16: the Greek word *Parakletos*, which is translated "Counsellor" in the NIV, but actually means "One who stands at our side in order to help."

Come back to my incompetence at cricket. The only use for my batting is to provide a distraction for the opposing team, with the hope that some of them might become incapacitated through too much laughter! However, imagine if it were possible for the cricketing skill of a very great batsman, like the England captain Graham Gooch, to live in me when I go to the wicket; then when I batted it would not be my skill but Graham Gooch's skill inside my body. That would make the opposition sit up!

Of course, this is impossible on a natural level. But it is exactly what Jesus has done by giving us the Holy Spirit. He knows that we can never live the Christian life on our own. So he has sent the Holy Spirit in order that, as we learn to "walk by the Spirit," Jesus will live in us, changing us from miserable failures to men and women who are able to live like he did.

Spiritual Fruits

The result of living in the Spirit is that the character of Christ begins to grow in us. Left to ourselves, our own sinful nature produces a horrible list of vices which Paul outlines in Galatians 5:19–21: sexual immorality, impurity and debauchery; idolatry and witchcraft; hatred, discord, jealousy, fits of rage, selfish ambition, dissensions, factions and envy; drunkenness, orgies, etc. These are things which are all too common in our world today; we see them headlined every time we pick up a newspaper.

Unfortunately, they are far too often seen within some churches. Instead of the peace and harmony Christ intends, there are quarrels, factions and cliques. A spirit of materialism and selfishness has replaced love and sacrifice. Christians, instead of being "in the world but not of it," are too often "of the world but not in it"!

The reason is that, instead of living by the Spirit,

people are living according to their old nature, and, "When the old nature is alive, the devil plays a thousand tunes on us."[11] Paul gives us a solemn warning: if we live like this we will not inherit the kingdom of God.[12]

Such living is a travesty of what the church is about. To quote a well-known Christian poster, "God want spiritual fruits, not religious nuts." Instead of living by our natural instincts, God wants us to put them to death and live with the Spirit in charge. Then our characters will start conforming to the wonderful list of spiritual fruit which make up the character of Christ: "love, joy, peace, patience, kindness, goodness, faithfulness, gentleness and self-control" (Gal 5:22–23).

Spiritual Relationships

In order to develop this "fruit" in us, God does not take us out of the world and put us into monasteries so that, being cut off from other human beings, we might learn to be spiritual. Rather, he puts us together with other human beings, in churches, families and places of work, to teach us through the "School of Life"; and it is these very relationships which he uses to shape our character. For example, if you are praying for patience, God may teach you patience by sending along some aggravating individual or circumstance. You then have to practise patience!

Fortunately, we are not alone here either. Before giving the Ephesian Christians instructions on relationships, Paul tells them to "be filled (and keep being filled) with the Spirit" (Eph 5:18). The Holy Spirit is given to us to stand alongside us and teach us to live in relationship with each other.

This is not easy. We all know only too well the tensions that can exist in modern family life; or the problems we can have at work where we are surrounded by people whose values and lifestyle are very different from our own. However, the glorious news is that the resurrected Christ is with us just as much when we are at home or at work as when we are in church.

It is tragic when Christians develop spiritual schizophrenia; they are one thing at church but another when they are at home, college or at work. In my early years as a schoolteacher, I used to find it difficult to find much fulfilment in what I was doing. Weren't the hours I spent teaching physics a waste of time, time that could be better spent studying the Bible or praying?

However, I then made a wonderful discovery. Jesus was just as interested in my schoolteaching as he was in my praying! I could therefore ask the Holy Spirit to help me in the classroom—no small comfort with a difficult class! What's more, I learnt that the person whom I had to please in my teaching was not my headmaster, but Jesus Christ!

This wonderfully changed my whole attitude to my job, and, though I was never the most gifted schoolteacher, I was a far more successful, not to mention contented, one. What's more, my opportunity for witness at the school dramatically increased!

I have many times shared this with people who have been members of the churches I have pastored. I remember one man telling me of the terrible frustration he had with his job. I told him what I had found as a schoolteacher, and within a few months he told me he was completely fulfilled in his work. What's more, he was soon on the list for promotion! The difference?

Instead of struggling on his own, he had taken the power of the risen Christ to work with him.

This power for living is also available to the young person at school or college, where peer pressure to conform to a set image is so strong. And Jesus will make our homes better places for both ourselves and our children if we will but conform to his pattern laid down in Ephesians 5:22–6:4. This is only possible by the radical life of the Holy Spirit working within us.

There are too many Christian families feeling the pressures of the materialism and lax morals of our modern society. As a result, the home life of both parents and children is very different from the image they project when at church. When the minister of a large and very successful church died, many tributes were paid at his funeral. But the greatest compliment paid was by his son who simply said that his father was exactly the same man at home as he was in the pulpit. The power of the Spirit was present in his living just as in his preaching.

Spiritual Witness

By having Christ with us in our ordinary, everyday lives, we shall be a witness to those whom we come into contact with. Isn't it amazing, that with all our modern sophistication, with our many excellent seminars and books on evangelism, our success in the West does not compare with the early church; nor, for that matter, with Christians in the third world who have little access to most of what we would deem as essential to modern evangelism.

The simple fact is that, while great televised

crusades, literature, videos, and all our modern trappings have their place, it is the actual lives of Christians which speak most to people. Jesus told his disciples, "You shall receive power when the Holy Spirit comes upon you; and you will be my witnesses...to the ends of the earth" (Acts 1:8). The rapid spread of the Gospel is a testimony to their success. Filled with the Spirit, they witnessed, in their lives, their words and with supernatural signs and wonders that Jesus was alive. People saw Jesus in them.

The word "witness" refers to someone who has first hand knowledge of an event. Through the Holy Spirit, we can all have a first hand knowledge of the power of the risen Christ working within us. Then, as we witness in the world, people shall see that Jesus is in us. One problem with the Western church is that we have too much teaching and too little personal experience of spiritual matters.

Compare the pastor's wife whom I had the privilege of meeting in India. Explaining how they reached the primitive "Hill-tribe" people, her evangelistic strategy was simple but remarkably effective: "We go to these people and hold a meeting in their village. As we start singing about the blood of Jesus, those who are demon-possessed start reacting. We then cast out the demons, preach the Gospel, pray for the sick, and start a church in the village".

The conversion of the heathen does not lay in sophisticated evangelistic methods; rather a demonstration of the power of the risen Christ, accompanied by signs and wonders. It is the rediscovery of this same power in the lives of ordinary believers that will herald a major turning to God in the Western world.

Spiritual Warfare

Imagine two first century armies lined up against each other—Rome and one of its enemies. Each soldier stands, nervous but eager, wanting to do his best for his king. At the signal, javelins dipped in tar and lighted are thrown, inflicting heavy damage to those not keeping their shield in place. Then, at the signal, the two armies charge towards each other, and are soon locked in vicious hand-to-hand fighting, with no quarter given.

Is this a scene from a Hollywood epic? No—rather the scene Paul had in mind when he wrote the section on spiritual warfare in Ephesians 6. For Paul, the Christian life was not all plain sailing, any more than it was for Jesus himself. Jesus warned his disciples about the problems and difficulties they would face living in this world; not just the ordinary trials and heartaches of everyday life, but problems stemming directly from the fact that they were Christians.[13] Similarly, the apostles instructed their converts, "We must go through many hardships to enter the kingdom of God" (Acts 14:22).

The fact is that the Christian has a great and powerful enemy who opposes him at every point. The Bible tells us that, however difficult men and circumstances may be, "Our struggle is not against flesh and blood, but against the rulers, against the authorities, against the powers of this dark world and against the spiritual forces of evil in the heavenly realms" (Eph 6:12).

The enemy is named Satan, the devil. He is known variously as "the prince of this world",[14] "the accuser of the brothers",[15] "the prince of the power of the air".[16] He hates God and everything to do with God's kingdom and he and his army of demons are "hell-bent" on the spiritual ruin of every Christian.

Therefore, from the day of his conversion, the Christian is in a terrible battle with the powers of evil. He is called to be a soldier until the day he arrives in heaven. Paul tells his young companion, Timothy, to "Fight the good fight of the faith"[17] and to "Endure hardship with us like a good soldier in Christ Jesus".[18] Paul would have had little time for the modern idea of the church as a "healing centre for sick souls" with endless sympathetic counselling available. The apostle does not call us to a clinic or rest home—rather to a barracks and a battlefield! We are not called to wallow in our problems—rather to stand like men and defeat the enemy!

However, defeating the enemy is far from easy. He is out to give us a hard time and knows nothing of "Queensberry Rules" or "Geneva Conventions". I have known many people ask me, "Why have I had all these problems since becoming a Christian?" My answer is always the same: 'You now have an enemy." However, I am quick to add, "But God has given you the means to defeat him!"

In order to stand against the devil, it is vital we know the tactics he uses to to discourage the Christian from following Christ. Here are just a few of them:

Temptation: often, a Christian will feel a much stronger temptation to sin. This is partly because he is more aware of sin, but also because the devil is now giving him special treatment. The devil's strategy is to tempt the Christian to sin, and then accuse his conscience by saying, "You're a fine Christian, sinning like that!"

False Doctrine: Satan is a master of twisting the Scriptures, often so near but so far from the truth.[19] This is the reason for so many false cults in the world. The

Christian must take care that he does not get side-tracked, for to get "hooked" on a false teaching will severely limit his usefulness to God.

Attacks on the mind: all sorts of doubts, fears and even blasphemies can arise in our minds, together with harsh thoughts about our families or fellow Christians.

Hostility from the world: Jesus told his disciples to expect the hatred of men because they were Christians.[20] One of the first things a new Christian notices is that often people who were his friends turn hostile when he tells them about Christ. Therefore he experiences opposition and even persecution from the world. However, this does not have its origin in men: it is rather the hostility raised up by Satan against the Christian.

How do we fight this mighty foe? The first principle to realise is that Jesus, by his death and resurrection, has overcome Satan once and for all; he has destroyed the power of the devil.[21] Satan may at present appear to be all-powerful on this earth, but the reality of it is that, since Calvary, he is like a serpent writhing in his death-throes.[22] Hence, the Christian who is walking with God will overcome the devil in the same way as Jesus did.

However, we must not rely on our own strength. We overcome with the power of God: "Be strong in the Lord, and in his mighty power" (Eph 6:10); and by putting on "the full armour of God" (Eph 6:13–17) we are protected against the worst Satan can do. The power comes to us through prayer in the Spirit (Eph 6:18); and we put on the armour by knowing the great doctrines contained within the Word of God, the Bible, particularly those relating to justification by faith. Such a soldier, strong and fully armed, will be able to stand

his ground against Satan's attacks, and when the battle
is over, he will still be standing. Of course, this means
that his enemy will *not* be left standing![23] He will
have taken to his heels and fled, just like he did with
Jesus.[24]

Through the power of the risen Christ we can meet
this fearsome foe and defeat him, even in the face of
death itself.[25] But the extent of that power depends on
just how close we walk with God. To help us in our
walk with him, God has given us those who will spiritually build us up.

Spiritual Input

In the fellowship of the local church, God has given us
those who will pray, fellowship, and break bread with
us; also men gifted by himself who have the ability to
expound the scriptures in a fashion that will build us up
as Christians.[26] The New Testament views church life
not as an optional extra for an hour on a Sunday
morning, but as the lifeblood of the believer. The early
Christians realised the importance of fellowship: they
"devoted themselves to the apostles' teaching and to
the fellowship, to the breaking of bread and to prayer"
(Acts 2:42).

It is of uttermost importance for every Christian to
be involved with a strong, Bible-based local church,
which preaches and practises the power of the risen
Christ. Through the church he can be built up and
encouraged, trained to live the Christian life in the
world.

It is therefore tragic when Christians show little
desire for church life. This is completely contrary to
what is taught in the New Testament, which tells us

"Let us not give up meeting together, as some are in the habit of doing, but let us encourage one another — and all the more as you see the Day approaching" (Heb 10:25).

At a meeting of ministers I attended, several men confessed that their congregations lost interest in the sermon if it went on for more than ten minutes. No wonder so many Christian lives are a failure! There was something wrong, either with the preachers or, more likely, with the spiritual appetites of the hearers! As the old saying goes: "Sermonettes produce Christianettes."

Compare that with the pattern of the early church.[27] Or of the various revivals in church history, when the church has really functioned in the power of the Spirit. Christians came out of church meetings, not only eager to get back again, but also as vibrant witnesses to Christ in the world about them.

It is as we recapture the importance and centrality of life in the Spirit-filled local church, that we shall be better equipped for life in the world around us. Then together we will start being that city on a hill that cannot be hidden.[28]

Spiritual Joy

Is this life miserable? Restrictive? Not according to the early Christians. The early chapters of Acts are filled with vibrancy and elation about their Christian experience that came directly from knowing the risen Christ. We see them eating together "with glad and sincere hearts, praising God".[29] When Philip preaches the gospel in Samaria there is "great joy in that city"[30] and an Ethiopian who accepts Christ goes "on his way rejoicing".[31] Even when Paul and Silas are beaten and put in a stinking dungeon they sing praises to God!

We get this same feeling of joy in the letters. Paul uses the word "joy" no less than twenty-three times, and tells his converts: "Rejoice in the Lord always. I will say it again: Rejoice!" (Phil 4:4) Was this because life was so much easier for them? No! Often the letters are written to people under persecution. But in spite of their many trials, they were "filled with an inexpressible and glorious joy" (1 Pet 1:8).

What is the root cause of this wonderful joy? It is the joy of being a member of the greatest thing in the universe—the kingdom of God. That kingdom, ruled by the risen Christ, is "righteousness, peace and joy in the Holy Spirit" (Rom 14:17).

That joy should be the hallmark of every Christian today, because the power of Jesus' death and resurrection is the same today as it was at the beginning. This power enables us to be "more than conquerors",[32] and turns the Christian life into a wonderful and vital adventure for God.

11

God's Final Purpose

Finally, we must remember, God's purpose for us is not the trials and struggles of this earth, but the glory of heaven. Then we shall see Jesus. He will be the only being in heaven whose looks are less than perfect; for throughout eternity he will carry the scars of his death for us. When we see those scars, we shall realise something of the cost of what he did for us by his death and resurrection; and we shall fall down before him in wonder, and shall sing with the great company of heaven,

"Worthy is the Lamb, who was slain,
to receive power and wealth and wisdom and strength
and honour and glory and praise!"

(Rev 5:12)

Notes for Part 3

1. See *I Believe in the Church* (Hodder) for David Watson's radical solution.
2. Mt 5:13–14
3. Mt 5:16
4. Mt 16:18–19
5. 1 Thess 1:6

6. Rom 8:37
7. Lk 22:54–62
8. Gal 2:11–21
9. In Bible times baptism was always by full immersion.
10. Acts 2:33
11. Often quoted in Eric Maddison, whose book, *Are you missing God's Best?* is published by Lifestream.
12. Gal 5:21
13. Jn 15:18–25
14. Jn 14:30
15. Rev 12:10
16. Eph 2:2 (KJV)
17. 1 Tim 6:12
18. 2 Tim 2:3
19. See Lk 4:1–13
20. Jn 15:18–25
21. Col 2:15; Heb 2:14
22. Rev 12:12
23. Eph 6:13
24. Lk 4:13; Jas 4:7
25. Rev 12:11
26. Eph 4:11–16
27. For example Acts 20:7
28. Mt 5:14
29. Acts 2:46–47
30. Acts 8:8
31. Acts 8:39
32. Rom 8:37